In support of *Lyri*
A New Dimension in Exp̶r̶e̶s̶s̶i̶v̶e̶ ̶M̶u̶s̶i̶c̶i̶a̶n̶s̶h̶i̶p̶

"Ed ... I have greatly enjoyed reading and rereading your newest book, *LYRICAL CONDUCTING*, in which you accurately diagnose our less than effective ability to teach musical expressivity at ALL levels. The insight and suggestions you offer in the book are wonderful. Only someone with the exceptional experience and consummate musicianship of Ed Lisk could have given us the great gift of this book. THANK YOU!"

JOHN WHITWELL, Director of Bands Emeritus, University Distinguished Professor, Michigan State University

"Wow, even more powerful than your earlier publications. I just think the essay does a masterful job of stating the problem and then providing possible solutions. Your techniques for developing expression in conductors are groundbreaking, Ed. I have been using them with all of my conductors, and myself, and it is making a tremendous difference."

DR. KENNETH OZZELLO, Director of Bands, University of Alabama

"Ed Lisk goes beyond the conventional methods of teaching. By doing so, he provides ways to produce exceptional individuals and ensembles. It isn't just about what we ask of ourselves or of our players, but how we ask. Not just telling them how to make a phrase, but empowering them to step out and take a risk and creating an environment to take that risk.

During the past thirteen years, Ed Lisk has worked with me in rehearsals with the Clarence Wind Ensemble. I have witnessed each and every word of this book come alive. No one today that speaks about the mysteries of expression and music making and puts it into practical usable terms the way Ed Lisk has. This is a must read (along with his other books) for anyone in or going into the music education profession."

WILLIAM EICHER, Director of Bands, Clarence High School Wind Ensemble, Clarence, NY

"The first time I attended Edward S. Lisk's session, I experienced one of those moments where everything I had been trying to convey for years to myself and my students became crystalline and real, and the words and ways in which to approach my teaching became transparent. As Ed taught us about the interconnectedness of each individual in mind/body/spirit was put into words, motion, and music."

ELIZABETH SOKOLOWSKI, Chair of Music Education, University for the Arts, PA

"I just finished reading your chapters on lyrical conducting and thoroughly enjoyed seeing your mind at work. THIS IS GREAT STUFF! You are so on target when you point out that the best conductors (musicians!) conduct the phrase lines … not the patterns! Your writings on the *art* of conducting are spot on … absolutely BRILLIANT!"

PAULA CRIDER, Director Emeritus,
University of Texas Bands

"What a great approach to expressive conducting … and the concepts are seemingly so simple. Yet, we don't teach like that and should. Congratulations, and once again, great quotes from your many sources. Thank you for sharing this with me. Bravo!"

FRANK B. WICKES, Director of Bands Emeritus,
Lousiana State University

"To my colleagues in the public schools I encourage you to read this book; read it again, reflect on the words, and read it yet again, for BETWEEN the words are beautiful ideas that will change your own definition of the role of the teacher-conductor forever. In my years seeking to understand Mr. Lisk's musical mind, this has been my experience and I will be forever grateful."

TOM DAVIS, Composer, Director of Bands, Canandaigua City School
District, Canandaigua, NY

"It is so stimulating to read the things you write … something of substance that makes me think about things in a new way. You have done a great job of demystifying the natural laws of expression. Ed, this is another great contribution to our professional literature. You take on the tough topics that are so important for all of us."

LARRY R. BLOCHER, Ph.D., Professor and Director,
School of Music, Troy University

"Your "Lyrical Conducting" is the clearest, most concise description of expressive musicianship I have ever seen. As you note, many authorities have described details of certain elements of expressiveness, but you have synthesized cogent points into a single presentation that provides cohesive understanding.

Currently, the profession seems to be obsessed with workshops, clinics, etc., on physical techniques of conducting and mechanics of achieving ensemble accuracy of pitch, rhythm and markings, but those sessions overlook the fundamental issue of musical sensitivity and personal possession of expression that is to be brought from the innermost soul communicated to the ensemble by conducting.

Thank you for letting me read your work. "Lyrical Conducting" has so much valuable content that I could go on and on, but will stop for now."

DR. DAVID MCCORMICK, Secretary, Midwest Clinic Board of Directors

Lyrical CONDUCTING

A NEW DIMENSION IN EXPRESSIVE MUSICIANSHIP

EDWARD S. LISK

Published by
Meredith Music Publications
a division of G.W. Music, Inc.
1584 Estuary Trail, Delray Beach, Florida 33483
http://www.meredithmusic.com

MEREDITH MUSIC PUBLICATIONS and its stylized double M logo are trademarks of
MEREDITH MUSIC PUBLICATIONS, a division of G.W. Music, Inc.

Cover and text design: Shawn Girsberger

International Standard Book Number: 978-1-57463-220-0
Cataloging-in-Publication Data is on file with the Library of Congress.
Library of Congress Control Number: 2012956083
Printed and bound in U.S.A.

Contents

Introduction

On the podium ...

Patterns and gestures, at what point is musical meaning created? Does musical meaning and expression come from the physical movement of patterns and gestures or some inner source of our being? What is this source that prompts such movements?

As we prepared to enter this profession, patterns and gestures were the priorities as we learned the fundamentals of conducting. Unfortunately, less time was devoted to conducting musical expression or "felt meaning." Too often, we became consumed with the "mechanics of meaning" while never experiencing the "risk" or "truth" in musical expression. It was much easier to go the "analytical route" and much more difficult to take the "expressive" route. Perhaps we lacked the confidence or belief in our own interpretations, or the awareness that we have the power to interpret music and it's meaning through our conducting. This condition exists primarily because musical expressivity was seldom addressed in our preparation in becoming a conductor.

Our instructional techniques have taught us how to apply the signs and symbols of sound, leaving behind the finite details of what makes music expressive. Many attempts have been made to define artistry, expression, and the mysteries of music's finest detail, and yet the answers remain elusive. Perhaps this publication will bring you closer to an answer.

As conductors, we must search our souls to discover the truth and meaning of music as we guide ensembles to the pinnacle of expression. Our perceptions and self-awareness of the intangibles of music compliments our conducting skills. This dictates the quality of our performance that leads to value, worth, and appreciation. Without truth and integrity, more often than not, our results lead to contrived imitation.

My search and desire to compile this publication is coming at a point in my career that has provided me with extensive experiences through teaching and conducting. It is my intense desire to document my thoughts and music making procedures through the many enriching years of joy I was fortunate to experience as a musician, teacher, and conductor. The opportunities of sharing and giving alongside many of the legends in our profession provided me with an education that has been priceless. Their giving and sharing, through the depths of musical performance, made me what I am today as a musician.

This text is in three parts. Part 1, *Lyrical Conducting*, documents my approach to conducting and a means to enhance our lyrical approaches to conducting techniques. Lyricism is a top priority in conducting. Too often, we observe conductors who lack "lyricism" in their style and their interpretation of musical performances. The body language of conducting requires poise and finesse in what we are expressing visually. In this section, you will have many considerations regarding your thoughts and techniques for conducting.

In Part 2, I address *Interpretation: Looking Beyond Notation* and how we develop our personal or unique rendering of a composition. I place considerable emphasis on breaking away from conventional methods that frequently create contrived, or imitated renditions of literature. If artistic performance is our goal, it is necessary to have a performance vocabulary and reservoir of artistic considerations to rely on. It is the conductor's distinctive personal vision of a piece of music based on his or her knowledge and extensive performance experience that is the foundation of interpretation. Hopefully, this section will stimulate you to expand your "artistic vocabulary."

Part 3 addresses *Emotions and Music Making.* Emotions receive little attention because of its vagueness and depth. It is our emotional response that shapes the beauty and expressive qualities of our interpretation and conducting. Our emotions are the result of our life and musical experiences.

As my writings indicate, many of my concepts and instructional techniques trigger new and different considerations for what we do as teachers and conductors of instrumental music. Throughout my musical life, I looked beyond convention and tradition. I felt different from my musical friends. I always heard things differently and my answers to my teachers and professors were quite different from other classmates. It seemed that I simply could not fit into the "frameworks" of what was considered standard or conventional. My answers were always from a different perspective. I share these differences with you because as you read this publication you may be wondering where ALL of THIS came from.

Many notable conductors who have read parts of this publication have informed me that the areas that I present are simply "groundbreaking." If you have read my previous publication, you understand that my ideas depart from many of the conventional methods.

My desire with this publication is only to attempt to expand your awareness with the beauty of musical expression and its direction for greater musical meaning.

"Artistic expression has no limitations.
It is spontaneous and cannot be programmed or imitated.
Artistic expression is freedom...
Freedom from preconceived patterns or boundaries.
Once expression is 'programmed,'
it no longer exists as artistic expression."

—EDWARD S. LISK, 2012

A basic conducting technique should be in place before undertaking the lyrical patterns and approaches presented. The words and statements that follow are one man's opinion on musical expression based on over 50 years of music making.

PART I

CHAPTER

1

Lyrical Conducting

"Music making begins in the mind, not in the stick."

—LEONARD BERNSTEIN

*"We tend to be inhibited by the printed score with its scarcity of
expressive markings. There are so many excellent instrumentalists
who are completely obsessed by the printed note, whereas it has a
very limited power to express what the music actually means."*

—PABLO CASALS

We entered the world of music making at an early age. The mystery of
musical satisfaction and joy prompted countless hours of practice.
The *flame* of musical expression, passion, and excitement continued to
expand until it consumed a life devoted to the mysteries that surround
music making. After devoting years of study and practice, we became
music teachers. We were dedicated and determined to share the beauty of
music with students.

After my more than 50 years of music making, I finally realized that
one must truthfully experience artistry in order to teach and share this state

of performance. It is my opinion that conventional methods frequently create barriers and restrict expressivity. When we observe a conductor with eyes focused on the score, and strictly adhering to *patterns,* the musical result and focus on attention has no connection to the meaning that exists beyond the markings on the printed page. Instead, a sterile and note-perfect rendering is the outcome. The same is true when listening to a soloist that abides by every dynamic, accent, legato marking, etc. But, is it music?

The differences are based on how one perceives the intangibles and subtleties surrounding the beauty of musical notation. This awareness is the result of knowledge, study, and experience. This elusive area of music study is intriguing and perpetuates our search for answers.

A musician looks beyond the obvious. He or she has an imagination different from others. The ability to see the invisible expressive elements surrounding notation and to uncover the expressivity of the composer is a unique characteristic. The same musical imagination is engaged as we view the beauty found in a painting, architecture, or in other forms of art. For example, as you look at the picture below, are you able to see the rhythmic patterns, melodic flow, and harmonic content in the design of this building?

This observation simply expands a person's imagination as they look beyond the obvious to make artistic connections. I believe when we live a life of *music,* we see *music* in all things that surround our every day experiences. Something that truly enlightens directors who attend my sessions is when I speak about the *rhythm of the room.* I point out the various patterns of floor tiles, the spacing of lights, and windows,

and any other designs that are easily viewed as *rhythm* and note values. I often will clap or chant those rhythms; I see *music* in all my surroundings.

Music expresses an individual's soul and passion. Whereas, contrived expression is superficial, lacking meaning and depth. A musician's intelligence is the accumulation of artistic expression and considerations that have evolved over years of practice and deep understanding. This is the difference between an average performance and an artistic performance. The artistic performance is immersed in the truth and integrity of spontaneous expression. Such a performance *elevates* the musician, conductor, and audience; it is the mystery of music that sends chills up our spine. It is a product of a life filled with solitude, study, practice, and performance experience.

The significant factor that makes our music's greatness is the depth of our musicianship. H. Robert Reynolds had this to say about depth, *"A person of very shallow musicianship can actually conduct Irish Tune quite well, and have it come out nicely. Someone with greater musical depth can bring out more of its depth. The problem is that you can't really become a deeper musician if you only are acquainted with pieces at your own depth. You have to be acquainted and work with pieces of greater depth than you are ready for at that time."* Musical shallowness has no place in a musician's mind.

CHAPTER

2

Looking Beyond Conventional Methods

"Conductors who communicate the affective qualities of the music are always more successful than those who communicate only technical details. It is the feeling behind the "how" that makes all the difference in the world to the musicians and ultimately to the audience."

—JAMES MURSELL

We have all viewed and heard memorable concerts by the *masters* of conducting. A few of the wonderful orchestral conductors that I enjoy observing are, Leonard Bernstein, Seija Ozawa, Gustavo Dudamel, George Szell, Claudio Abbado, Ricardo Muti, Carl St. Clair, and Arturo Toscanini, to name a few. As we observe these unique individuals, what is most apparent is the fact that their conducting is quite different from many wind band conductors. The biggest difference is that these master conductors are totally immersed with the flow of music being created by the orchestra. This is not to say that wind band conductors are not, only that wind band conductors tend to focus on pattern oriented motions, cueing, and preprogrammed moves.

The most notable difference with these masters is how their spontaneous response to the music shapes their movements and gestures. Their expressive gestures are connected to the lyricism and flow of the music. If a conducting pattern is used, it is usually slight and never intruding. Their moves are spontaneous. The face, arms, hands, and body language are connected and immersed in music. Their lyrical moves and expressive hand/body nuances would be impossible for anyone to repeat or imitate. Obviously, whenever these notable individuals conduct a composition, their conducting is unique to that composition and performance. I am totally convinced that their conducting styles are a natural physical and passionate occurrence of an inner image of the flowing musical lines being created by the orchestra.

I discovered through my research two distinct schools of thought about conducting. Leonard Bernstein stated that Mendelssohn fathered the elegant school, whereas Wagner inspired the passionate school of conducting. Gunther Schuller describes Mendelssohn's style of conducting *"as being informed by a basic fidelity to the score and historical, stylistic authenticity. Mendelssohn became a symbol of objective music-making, exposing classical clarity, and unity in performance."* In Frank Battisti's publication, On Becoming a Conductor, he states, *"Richard Wagner is generally credited with being the founder of the interpretive school of conducting. His style of conducting was molto expressivo. Wagner's performances featured fluctuation in tempo and a pulse that moved in phrases rather than bars. He exercised great domination over the orchestra."*

My conducting is a personal expressive and physical response to what I am hearing harmonically, melodically, and rhythmically *in the moment*. My physical response is generated by the ensemble's sound that dictates spontaneously what is passing through my mind and soul as I share my inner musical expression. Shaping of intrinsic expression evolves through countless hours of practice. Addressing the intensive and miniscule details of music is a fine art, crafted through time. The depth of what is beyond the obvious is where the truth of musical expression originates through honesty and not imitation.

As one observes notable orchestral conductors, it is obvious they are not consumed with any kind of pattern. If the mind is diverted to something other than the sound being created, the intense and immersed *connection* with music is lost. This immersed connection to the sound of music is extremely difficult to achieve. It requires a highly disciplined mind that is capable of focusing on the *whole and now* of music and time. This is what the word *immersion* means. If we stop and think, a pattern has no connection to feeling or expression. It usually is isolated and devoid of emotional thinking.

Early in my professional experiences as a clarinetist with the Syracuse Symphony Orchestra, I observed and discovered significant differences in how conductors engage an ensemble through music. Karl Kritz was my first conductor. He was a notable orchestral conductor from Austria. It was difficult to respond to his moves, as my training emphasized responding to typical conducting patterns. This new world of conducting for me was devoid of many patterns. When I removed my focus on conducting patterns, I realized to be a true musician I must respond to the entirety and sensitivity of orchestral sounds being guided by the conductor. With such a mental picture, musical flow, and lyricism evolved into beautiful, unrestricted musical expression. It was at this point in my professional career that I realized *pattern conducting,* more often than not, produced a paint-by-number response from the musicians. With a paint-by-number conductor, attention is focused to musical notation and its exactness rather than the beauty of musical lyricism. An *eye* response is the result when it should be an *ear* response.

Artistry: Beyond Notation

"Some believe that one should merely mechanically reproduce the
marks on the paper but I don't believe in that. We must defend the

composer against the mechanical conception of life, which is
becoming very strong today."

—LEOPOLD STOKOWSKI

Throughout my writings, I frequently speak about paint-by-number performances. Musical expression is not a paint-by-number exercise. Too often, we
fail to look beyond the specifics of notation. A literal interpretation produces a very sterile performance. After so many years of teaching and
making music, I realize that artistic expression can only be found in one
place. Artistic expression is found outside the boundaries of musical notation. To create an artistic performance requires taking the risk to venture
outside the restriction of notation. Our profession has not been conditioned
to take such risks, as it usually receives considerable criticism (adjudicators).
By taking the risk of going beyond notation, we discover where the "invisible" feelings of beauty, and passion are found. It is where others fear to go as
it involves a vulnerability of self and a display of pure emotion and
expression.

Music takes on a new meaning when we free ourselves from the restrictions of notation. We no longer are consumed with quarter, eighth, and
sixteenth notes, dynamic markings, accents, and so forth. Our mind is consumed with the sounds of lyrical phrases, harmonic and rhythmic content
shaping the whole and beauty of a performance. By taking risks, music is
no longer a mystery. Eloise Ristad stated in her wonderful publication,
*Soprano on Her Head, "When we withhold the fullness of our capabilities, we
diminish those capabilities. When we explore beyond where we feel safe and secure,
we discover abilities beyond our expectations."* It requires courage to step outside such boundaries, as we must spontaneously shape the musical
performance differently than how we were taught. This intuitive responsi-
bility of creating artistic flow is a heavy burden. It demands a confidence of
self and a belief and acknowledgement of how we feel, how the music
moves us and creates meaning. Such subjective analysis, beyond the frame-
work of the symbols and signs on the page, are a courageous path to

choose. The question becomes, do you have the courage to look beyond the unadorned markings and make beautiful music?

I use *America, the Beautiful* as an example when developing a uniqueness for musical expression.

As you physically see the notation for *America, the Beautiful*, if you look beyond the obvious (notes and rhythms), you will find where "feeling" and expression are hidden. Sing or play the song and see how expressive you can make it. If you perceive the exactness of the notation, it becomes a paint-by-number response.

The graphic at right represents a paint-by-number exercise. The illustration shows the rigidity of colors to be used within the boundaries or lines.

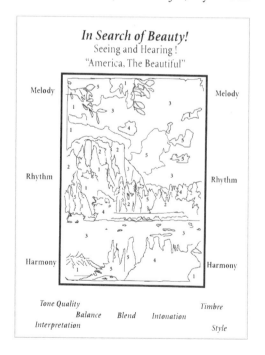

As you view the next graphic at right, it is apparent that the artist was not bound by lines, boundaries, or barriers of a paint-by-number exercise. The artist took the risk and went beyond those restrictions. The graphic represents the "whole" picture shaping the beauty of the scene.

In Search of Beauty!

The following illustration is intended to compliment your imagination as you relate and compare the pictures to a musical performance.

How a conductor perceives music beyond the obvious notation is what will dissolve those boundaries of notation. As the artist painted the above picture, his brush lifted off the canvas with no restrictions of lines. Gustav Mahler stated, *"What is best in music is not found in the notes."*

My professional experiences created an awareness of the differences between artistic thought versus automated/programmed moves. We can observe and hear the clear divide between prescription and passion. Perhaps, these are harsh statements, but I believe they must be said only to provide a different perspective on what we do. To be *connected* in this way, to the intensity of music, is no easy task. This is why music is often referred to as being mysterious.

Lacking Musical Expression

We have so many clinics, classes, symposiums, and workshops that attempt to address expressive conducting. Too often, there is very little that changes a conductor's approach as they quickly resort to what they normally have been doing. Not until an approach or method is implemented to connect musical sounds with the conductor's mind, soul, hands, arms, face, eyes, and body, will there be any change. Our external physical gestures must connect to the inner beauty of musical expression that emanates from the mind and soul. As these two elements converge, the truth of musical expression is found.

In our preparation to become band directors, the ability to teach musical expression is neglected. The ability to make musical meaning becomes contrived through *things* that are devoid of the feeling of expression. In my latest book, *The Musical Mind of the Creative Director*, I state, *"What I've learned is that the ultimate success formula for any band lies within the individual director. True musical education is about enhancing a musician's performance level through alerting their minds to the beauty of musical expression."*

As notable scholar David Whitwell states in his essay on *Music Education for the Future*, *"We are trained to talk about every kind of detail of notation and technique, but not feeling. Music Education has approached music as a technical discipline which can be taught and learned, but has left the most important part of music, its ability to communicate emotions and feelings, as an impenetrable mystery."*

While reading David Levitin's publication, *This Is Your Brain On Music*, you will find a frightening condition that exists in our universities today. On page 208, Dr. Levitin writes,

"So much of the research on musical expertise has looked for accomplishment in the wrong place, in the facility of fingers rather than the expressiveness of emotion. I recently asked the dean of one of the top music schools in North America about this paradox. At what point in the curriculum is emotion and expressivity taught? Her answer was that they aren't taught. "There is so much to cover in the approved curriculum, she explained, repertoire, ensemble, and solo training, sight singing, sight reading, music theory—that there simply isn't time to teach expressivity." David Levitin responded with, so how do we get expressive musicians? Her answer, "Some of them already come in knowing how to move a listener. Usually, they've figured it out themselves somewhere along the line." She further stated, "Occasionally, if there's an exceptional student, there's time during the last part of their last semester to coach them on emotion."

Another awakening study published in the Psychology of Music Journal, volume 36, *Musical Expression: An Observational Study of Instrumental Study*, by Jessika Karlsson and Patrik Juslin stated the following:

> Research has shown that both music students and teachers think that expression is important. Yet, we know little about how expression is taught to students. Such knowledge is needed in order to enhance teaching of expression. The aim of this study was thus, to explore the nature of instrumental music teaching in its natural context, with a focus on expression and emotion. Results suggested that the focus of teaching were mainly on technique and on the written score. Lessons were dominated by talk, with the teacher doing most of the talking. Issues concerning expression and emotion were mostly dealt with implicitly rather than explicitly, although some teachers used a variety of strategies to enhance expression. Although there were individual differences among teachers, a common feature was the lack of clear goals, specific tasks, and systematic teaching patterns.

David Whitwell writes in his essay, *On Movement and Music*,

> "When oratory became a discipline, early teachers of oratory all stressed the relationships between oratory, gesture and music. What they meant by that was that, like the musician, the orator must emotionally move his listeners. And so, to this very day, teachers of oratory discuss the broad subject of the emotional connection with the audience. This does not happen in music studies. The music teacher does not discuss how to move the feelings of the listener. That is, emotions in music are not taught as the natural purpose and object of music communication, but only as an element of individual technique. The

central purpose of music is to communicate feeling to a listener, yet we do not teach this."

These statements encourage us to reflect upon and to ponder the reprioritization of what we teach about musical expression and why we teach it. If we accept the statement that music communicates emotion, how will emotion be taught to young instrumental students? More importantly, how will we conduct and shape musical expression? There are no shortcuts for developing artistic expression. As Wilhelm Furtwangler stated, *"The mystical side of music is called emotional ... we're talking about the conductor's charisma... "Either you have it or you don't."* We cannot overlook James Jordan's significant statement, *"If one believes that music is self-expression, then it should follow that one must have a self to express."*

As a side note, a similar condition exists in how we teach listening and how students make musical decisions. I don't ever recall a class, clinic, or course where the clinician addressed what the student is listening to, what they are listening for, and what do they do with it after hearing it. Listening is a difficult skill to teach. This is why so many rely on strobe-tuners. In fact, we are so advanced with technology that we can clip a tuner to the instrument. I see our current system of playing in tune as being one of the two greatest weaknesses in our profession. The second is how we teach musical expression.

Do we have any technology on the horizon that will be used for creating spontaneous musical expression? Yes. Computer technology and software to measure expressivity are in the beginning stages of development. Currently, Neuroscientist David Levitin at McGill University has a highly sophisticated piano connected to a computer that measures and reproduces the subtle nuances and expressivity of a pianist. Additional software will soon be available to measure expressivity with other wind instruments. Does this mean that we will soon hear duplicate performances of some of our most virtuoso soloists? Will this eventually suppress natural, spontaneous artistic expression?

The Mystery of Musical Expression

"Notes, like words, are mere utterances of symbols, and within themselves are totally lacking and incapable of expression. It is the human response, not the mechanical one that created the communication between the written symbol, the performer and the listener."

—WILLIAM D. REVELLI

Leonard Bernstein conducts what the music communicates to him, and not something he has programmed. His profound statements, *"Music making begins in the mind and not the stick,"* and *"it is what you listen to just before it happens,"* are significant insights for our profession. His knowledge of the score lives inside his soul. He projects his love for shaping Mozart, Mahler, Brahms, or Beethoven through his conducting. This is not accomplished through prepared and prescribed conducting moves. Another *awakening statement* made by H. Robert Reynolds in a conducting symposium was, *"we learn a basic conducting pattern and hang all the music on that pattern."*

We have all attended a rehearsal and heard the conductor say, *follow me*, or *I want all eyes looking at me.* Those statements have nothing to do with creating musical expression. If I follow you, I will be late as time is *now*. Time does not follow an event. Time IS the event! If you want me to look at you, what am I supposed to see? Does this mean my attention is now focused on you, and not the music being made? These certainly are troubling statements, focused on the eye and not the ear! There is nothing wrong with such statements if we are conducting paint-by-number exercises.

Programmed conducting is not artistic or expressive conducting. Once conducting is programmed, it no longer exists as creative artistic spontaneity. Artistic integrity and passion are what make the memorable and humble musical moments we experience when attending concerts. It is very easy to sense contrived expression or imitation.

The Beauty of Silence

SILENCE! This is my space where I communicate
with my instrument . . .
just as an artist has canvas and a poet has paper. I experience my innermost
thoughts and feelings through sound
moving in and out of silence.
I carefully place my sound in this space of silence with a delicate touch of sound
and rhythmic stroke of color . . . This is my musical gift!

Throughout my musical life as a conductor and educator, silence was critical to my artistic considerations when conducting or playing an instrument. Silence surrounds musical sounds. Music is sound moving in and out of silence! Silence is the gateway into the art of musical expression. As I share with the listener the expression of my musical thoughts, a beautiful melody results as my inner passion engages with the flow and sound of music moving in and out of silence.

An area that receives very little attention is rests (eighth, quarter, half, whole, etc.). The rest, or silence, usually indicates the release of a phrase or motif, the ending of a composition, or the end of one section transitioning into a new section of the composition. How a conductor responds to the silence of rests is an area that makes a huge difference in the musicality of the composition. If the silence of a rest is literally interpreted, we immediately fall into a sterile or mechanical response with little musical meaning. Consideration MUST be given to the resonance of the last note preceding the rest/silence. The conductor must consider the note preceding the silence of the rest to prepare for what will happen with the silence that precedes the next entrance. This is a massive "space" where musical decisions are made. I frequently state throughout my presentations that I'm not sure as to how large an eighth, quarter, half, or whole rest is if I am considering note resonance and decay. How I handle this decay determines the size of the rest.

Sound into Infinity

The concept, *"music is sound moving in and out of silence,"* is essential when teaching phrases and musicianship. The concept places the mind in a position with *what IS to occur* and *what happens AFTER it occurs!* This thoughtful action is created after an entrance and throughout the duration of a particular note, followed by how that note moves into silence. The concept directs the mind to focus on the horizontal flow of sound moving to the "right" side of a note. This is a powerful concept indicating a thoughtful-thinking energy moving to an approaching point that occurs simultaneously through musical decisions, not a series of separate events.

The *beginning of silence* concept provides artistic consideration for resonance and decay of notes moving into the space of silence indicated by a rest. Apply this concept where a *space of silence (rest or breath mark)* follows a phrase, fermata sign, end of a composition, or any similar point in music.

The musical results will elevate the ensemble's performance. This is also a departure from the "score order release" so often being used today.

Elizabeth Sokolowski, in her new publication, *Making Musical Meaning*, had this to say: *"I had to perform at the Kimmel Center in Philadelphia. It was the most resonate and warmest hall I had ever performed in. At the conclusion of one of the pieces we played as the final chord sounded, I thought to myself that although the sound to our ears was no longer audible, the energy of the sound remained, floating, soaring, and living through the hall for an amount of time that I could not quantify. I could only perceive it as infinite. Moving away from the analytical, music moving both through and in time in regard to creative/expressive potential must be considered."*

Elizabeth's statement was the result of this significant musical experience dealing with artistic considerations I presented in a graduate class she attended. Basically, it was the concept of *"Music is sound moving in and out of silence."* The ensemble that I was conducting simply took advantage of the resonance of the Kimmel Center for the Performing Arts. Very few consider this concept and its application when performing in such a beautiful hall. The beauty of this silence that *"remained, floating, soaring, and living through the hall,"* would not be possible if a conventional conductor cut-off was made for the ensemble to release the sound. This concept is simply an "artistic consideration" that receives very little discussion. You and your students will experience the same "feelings" by applying the sound into silence exercise I describe below in this chapter.

As musical sounds move in and out of silence, the mind must be sensitized to the beginning of sound (as it enters from silence) and the right side of sound (as it moves into silence). These are two critical points of an extended note, a phrase, or a rhythm pattern. The concept elevates and places the energy of thoughtful thinking into an extremely delicate position at the beginning of sound (entrance) followed by the right side (into silence) of the produced sound. Conventional rehearsal techniques too often consume musical thinking that is directed to entrances, with little thought to how notes end or move into silence resulting in the need for a conductor to cut-off or stop sound.

A term, which I never use in my rehearsals, is the word "cut-off." The word has many implications, and I don't believe it has any connection to artistic thought. However, this word permeates our profession, neglecting natural musical resonance. For me, the phrase "cut-off" implies my band members have no idea when to release a note and I must make a conducting action that will "cut the sound off." Moreover, the word implies the students are not thinking and are not in control of what they are doing. The word does not recognize the natural resonance or decay of a note as the conductor abruptly "cuts off the sound." I urge you to reconsider the phrase and its implications with musical thought.

I must add this very important consideration regarding the resonance and decay of notes. Consider the musical sounds produced by stringed instruments. When a string instrument plays *pizzicato,* or lifting the bow off the vibrating string, the body of the instrument continues to vibrate. It is impossible to stop this decaying sound. With wind instruments, we can stop the sound (sometimes with very unmusical results). This decaying string vibration is exactly what prompted this teaching technique that I now share with you. It simply was a beautiful way of playing phrases, endings, and many other musical considerations.

Playing orchestral transcriptions is perhaps the most important consideration for this rehearsal technique. I distinctly remember listening to clinicians speak about the difficulty bands had when playing orchestral transcriptions. My wind ensemble applied this technique with the many orchestral transcriptions I programmed. The musical results impressed many of our guest conductors.

A musical performance should not be similar to a picture *'painted by numbers'* by sacrificing personal expression in fear of *spilling* over the indicated lines (or what an adjudicator may say). *If an artist is able to control the beauty and color of a brush stroke being lifted off the white canvas surface, or the color disappearing into the white canvas of silence . . . shouldn't the musician have similar control of sound moving into the white of silence (a rest or the end of a composition)?*

The next musical exercise will allow the ensemble and director to experience the beautiful sounds that exist beyond the line or boundaries of musical notation ... *a new dimension in playing phrases and musical considerations dealing with artistic responses.* Note that the following musical example does not have a time signature or bar lines. Although the process does imply 4/4, 3/4, and 2/4 time followed by a whole note with a fermata sign.

The exercise is as follows:

- *Step 1.* The students are to count the exercise in the following manner with a quarter = 60 or less pulse:

- *Step 2.* Play the exercise through several keys using major chords while silently counting in the normal or traditional way (use the Circle of 4ths) while being certain to have a quarter rest after each note.

- *Step 3.* After playing the above example in the usual conducted way, eliminate the counting of the quarter rest on beats 4, 3, and 2, as described below.
- Consider the next two statements very carefully to gain the musical benefits with this departure from any conventional approach.

* The beat-number syllable before the rest is now extended and tapers into the rest.

* The rest is IMPLIED and 'felt' in tempo, but not counted by the beat number.

The entire ensemble carefully speaks the process as follows:

1. *1 – 2 – threeeee … the 'eeeeee' tapers/decays into the 'felt' 4th beat into silence.*

2. *1 – twoooooo … the 'ooooo' tapers/decays into the 'felt' 3rd beat into silence.*

3. *1 – onennnnnn … the 'nnnn' tapers/decays into the 'felt' 2nd beat into silence. Hollllllllddddd … the 'llllddd' tapers/ decay into silence (unmeasured duration).*

The illustration below will further clarify the counting process and the tapering of the beat:

(4) Implied   (3) Implied   (2) Implied
1 - 2 - threeeeeeeeeee......1 - twooooooooooo........Onennnnnnnnnn......Holddddddd

This teaching process gains control of the *right side* of the note as it decays into silence. The ensemble should practice counting the sequence several times in tempo. The word *'hold'* is extended and provides a natural duration and taper for the whole note into silence (as in the ending of a composition). *After the 'hold', the students breathe and sense together the next natural entrance of the sequence.* Emphasize the importance of implying the *'felt' beat of the rest.* You can extend or abbreviate the decay of sound as it moves into the silence of the rest. The rest will be larger if less decay is needed and more decayed if the rest is smaller. Musical interpretation is the priority when applying this technique to literature.

It is important to emphasize to students that this timed spoken feeling and thinking energy is the same response (mind-body connection) that must be projected through the instrument to achieve the musical result! Applying this process to literature establishes a unified ensemble interpretation of phrase releases and controlled decay of sound. You have complete control of a note duration as it diminishes into the silence of a rest!

Play the exercise and continue through the *Circle of 4ths* using major chords. To start the ensemble, the director must count aloud (quarter = 60) the process as indicated above, with the extended decay of the number and hold; then take a preparatory breath, in tempo, with the students to indicate their entrance for the exercise. Once students become comfortable with the concept and process, *do not conduct. Trust the timed 'ensemble thought' and they will naturally breathe together.* The results will be flawless.

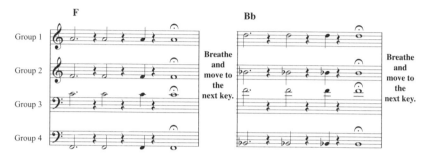

As students become comfortable with the exercise, repeat and have the students close their eyes while playing. The musical results improve significantly by using imagery. Playing with their eyes closed will intensify their thinking and remove any visual distractions that inadvertently may shift, or change focused concentration. The only preparatory action needed for the beginning of this exercise is that you "inhale" deeply so students will hear this inhale in tempo, similar to a preparatory beat with a baton. Instruct students to inhale deeply between each key change using the Circle of 4ths. The precision of the entire process (key to key) is based on internal ensemble pulse. You will be surprised as to the precise entrances and the duration of the decay into silence.

The success of this counting and thinking process is determined by *how the sound of counting the extended beat (before the rest) tapers or diminishes into the quarter rest of silence in order to control the musical result.* This same feeling and response is projected through the instrument! I understand the concern this will create with any traditional response to rests and our need to be specific and accurate with notation. *Understand, the time and pulse are still in place!* This rehearsal technique allows you to control the length of decay for tonal sonority and resonance similar to the wood body of a stringed instrument. This is a natural characteristic of all musical sounds.

Many traditional techniques dealing with articulation or conducting often disturb or clip the natural resonance, or decay of sound. This concept and exercise takes you beyond such unmusical reactions (and beyond the "paint by number" approach). This is another area where the beauty of expression is hidden within a musical performance. This process is similar to the analogy presented earlier ... *an artist is able to control the beauty and color of a brush stroke being lifted off and disappearing into the white canvas of silence. Musicians are NOW able to control the beauty of sound moving in and out of silence!*

This process should become a part of your rehearsal when shaping an artistic response to the natural decay of notes, chords, phrases, fermatas, or endings. I re-emphasize the controlling factor again, and that it is the energy of thought moving with sound into silence and 'feeling' this spoken decayed beat into silence. This does not require a 'cutoff' and should not be conducted. The ensemble becomes unified through timed thinking. This is the key to precision and accuracy. It is important to understand that the exercises are a natural occurrence with all musical sounds (unless the composer indicates the note should be abruptly cut off). Anything you do to change such a natural occurrence will be detrimental to the quality of your musical performance.

Location of Expressive Conducting

Does the mystery of music exist in this space of silence? I believe there are only three areas where the mystery of music can be found. The first is in the silence between beats. This is something very few speak about. It is where the conductor's musical direction and decisions are made, where the energy of musical thought is at its summit or peak, totally immersed in the *now of music making*. What musical decisions are happening between the spaces of silence between beats 1, 2, 3, or 4? If the mind is only consumed with the beats and notation, then music does not exist. It is simply an exercise, void of musical expression. Silence is where the mystery of music can be found. Isaac Stern states, *"Technique is not music ... Music is the thousandth of a millisecond between one note and another, how you get from one to the other - that's where the music is."*

The second area where the mystery of music is found is in the space between the conductor's eyes, face, body, and hands and the musicians seated before him/her. As I wrote in my last publication, the *energy of musical thought* passes through this space before the musicians and beyond the conductor. A conductor must project this energy of musical thought to communicate with freedom and unrestricted body language. Facial expressions complement all body movements in conveying intent and meaning. The nuance and inflection of musical phrases are a mind-body-soul connection with felt meaning and passion, projected through the sound of an instrument or the conductor's baton. Conducting movements must convey a similar meaning through the subtle nuance and inflection of face, body, and hands. This silent passionate movement of arms, hands, and fingers, coupled with facial expression, is the conductor's musical instrument. The thoughtful interpretation of written music, cradled within artistic feeling, guides conductors' physical movements as they project interpretation expressively through the silence of space before them, connecting to the musician's mind and response.

The third and final space is what goes on internally within the conductor's mind. A conductor is confronted with tremendous musical demands. Beyond the musical notation found in the score, the conductor is surrounded with sounds being created by the ensemble. He must balance countless musical details with the overall musical presentation. If the mind is consumed with analytical details, the music will not *live* or fulfill its purpose. The analysis lives during rehearsals and not in a performance. To create the musical entirety of the composer's intent, a conductor must be mentally elevated into a state of immersion. Such an immersed state removes all extraneous thoughts, including notation. We create the music! The music is not found in the score and the instruments have no intelligence! What we do with these tools is what brings music to life. The only thing remaining in the conductor's mind is the *whole* of musical sounds in the *now of time* (to be in the moment).

This state of mind is why we do what we do with music. This is what psychologist Mihaly Csikszentmihalyi speaks about in his publication, *Flow*. Flow is an optimal experience when we become so involved in what we are doing that the activity becomes spontaneous, almost automatic; we stop being aware of ourselves as separate from the actions we are performing. Csikszentmihalyi goes on further and states, *"Flow requires a highly disciplined mental activity. It does not happen without the application of skilled performance. Any lapse in concentration will erase it."*

Can this state of mind be taught? One must experience such a *state* before it is possible to place into an instructional setting. This mindset is something that jazz musicians have complete command of. As they play beautiful ballads, or other styles, they are totally immersed in the moment and have no other thoughts but to project their feeling of soul and passion. Notation is not a consideration. Charlie Parker states it best, *"If you don't live it, it won't come out of your horn. They teach you there's a boundary line to music. But man, there's no boundary line to art."*

Master Orchestral Conductors

"A conductor has two ways of communicating—facial expression and gesture, but the look in his eyes is often more important that the motion of a baton or the position of a hand."

—CHARLES MUNCH

arl St. Clair, conductor of the Pacific Symphony stated, *"How do you make notes into music? You must be able to look beyond the obvious. What are the clues?"* He goes on further to say, *"If you conduct musical moments as they happen, then you are directing the flow of music ... it's not the notation; it's the music."* Throughout my travels, I frequently state to directors, *"glide or soar over the top of the ensemble. Don't intrude upon the flow and energy of what is being produced. Don't conduct by imposition."* Of course, this is easy to say, but doing is impossible if you have not conditioned or rehearsed the ensemble. A unified perception of ensemble tone quality, time, tempo, dynamics, and the motion and energy of musical thought are essential basic elements. The musicians are responsible for the musical product that you, the conductor must shape.

Observing Leonard Bernstein conducting the ending of Mahler's 9th Symphony is truly an emotional experience. His movements reflect deep felt passion for the sounds being created. There are no patterns. Bernstein is simply pleading with outstretched hands that *touch* the sound, with total freedom supported by a whole body immersion. Bernstein's conducting would be hampered and destroyed if he ever thought of a conducting pattern in this setting. This was Bernstein's only way of communicating what inspired Mahler to create such a profound, intense musical experience.

Gustavo Dudamel is another conductor that is totally uninhibited on the podium. His conducting is very animated with embellished patterns. As he conducted the slow section of Dvorak's 9th Symphony, 4th movement, his moves were very lyrical. When he conducted the Beethoven's 5th Symphony, patterns were not evident. He had more vertical moves and in the lyrical sections, it was simply a slight pulse without patterns.

Claudio Abbado is totally immersed when conducting Mahler's Symphony #5. His body and facial expression are quite animated. Modified conducting patterns are slight and when the music demands, horizontal movements that flow as he appeals to the musicians with his left hand are utilized. Frequent large animated horizontal and vertical movements compliment the orchestra's performance.

Frank Battisti presents many examples of our most significant conductors throughout the history of music in his publication, *On Becoming a Conductor*. This is a *must-read* text for EVERY director in our profession. He cites the following quote:

> *"The stronger the imaginative powers of those who produce the music, the more potent the final result."* —Elizabeth Green

Gunther Schuller said, *"It is at that very highest level of performance that a wealth of interpretive choices and decisions became available at least to the really sensitive intelligent and imaginative re-creator. It is in this realm that there is not one pp, but many subtly different pp's ; not one f, but many different kinds of f's; not one slur but many kinds of legatos, etc. etc. The more basic point, however, is that it is pp, not a p or a mf!"*

The conductor's art of musical expression is a physical representation of what lies within his soul. When observing the masters, we see expressive, fluid, unobtrusive movements guiding the flow of sound from an ensemble. What is so wonderful about such conductors is the fact that if anyone attempts to imitate a master; he or she transforms what was once natural and flowing into something mechanical and sterile. It is clearly impossible to copy or imitate honesty, truth, respect, and passion. James Jordan states in his publication, *The Musician's Soul, "Being able to open oneself to the ensemble, to the audience or to the classroom makes an assumption that one can be open to oneself and vulnerable to the world at large. That is, the musician has the ability to be himself devoid of ego, and that he is able to travel to the place within himself where all impulses for making music live."*

Musical Decisions

"I did it my way."

—PAUL ANKA

Throughout my years of clinic and workshop presentations, I have observed that directors tend to be reserved when trying to conduct music expressively. Where does this inhibition come from? Having taught for over half a century at all levels, I believe that reservation and inhibition enter with our very first lesson in elementary or middle school and continues through high school and beyond. We always waited for our teacher to tell us that we played something correctly before we could move on to new material.

From our earliest instruction, teachers defined musical expression through a crescendo, decrescendo, phrase peaks, breath marks, and so on. We were graded for lesson preparation, and we did not dare to venture beyond the written notes and directions. Although we might have had different feelings about the phrase or melody, we were obliged to follow directions. Such a learning environment stifled any imagination or expression in the student and director. The goal of the learning was merely technical perfection, void of passion, and expression.

Another situation that plagues a director's conducting is the many years of practice focused on error-free performance when playing an instrument. This is obvious as all attention is directed to score, notes, rhythms, dynamics, and all the notation details. How often have we heard, *"get your head out of the score."* The result of such conducting creates a very sterile performance that seriously lacks in musical style and expression. I frequently refer to this as being a *paint-by-number exercise*, meaning we cannot go outside the boundaries or lines of notation. I believe that artistic expression lies outside the boundaries or lines. It is the *risk* we take to venture outside the boundaries of notation that allows us to create a beautiful performance or picture.

When students and directors have not had opportunities to exercise expression, their expressive ability atrophies, just as muscles weaken over years of neglect. To prevent this, it is important to develop rehearsal techniques that activate the student's emotional center and encourage feeling to flow through their instruments. Our emotional center controls and releases human feelings surrounding words and music, and when released fully, our emotional center determines the communicative actions of our conducting.

The uniqueness of musical thought is projected through the subtle, rhythmic nuance and inflection of note patterns that form a musical line or phrase. Nuance is the key that opens the door to the mysterious world of musical expression that has eluded teachers for so many years. Everyone has experienced deep sadness, excitement, quiet reflection, anxious moments, passionate feelings, and fear. These are but a few descriptors of our feelings that are portrayed through speech and voice. These are the nuances and inflections that I speak about in my publications. This is what shapes the uniqueness of our musical expression that is projected through our instrument or conducting. This is the application of *musical intelligence.*

Making Music Visible With Your Hands

Through my research, I discovered the notable Russian conductor and pedagogue, Ilya Musin. Musin guest conducted many distinguished Russian and European orchestras throughout the early 1900's, and in 1937, began teaching conducting at the Leningrad Conservatory. He held this position until his death in 1999 at the age of 95. Musin stated, *"The art of conducting lay in making music visible with your hands."* His approach required a physical relationship with the music as though one was sculpting sound. He taught his students to develop gestures that emerge from the emotional nature of the music and said, *"You have to feel the music, and you have to express its character and its emotion."* (Journal of the Conductors Guild, pg. 23, 24). In this same article, the great conductor Wilhelm Furtwangler, talks about the conductor's charisma. He stated, *"Either you have it or you don't. Charisma is innate. If it is there, Ilya Musin could develop it; if not, there is nothing you can do."* Musin further stated, *"A perfect technique or language is useless and empty, unless you have something to communicate to the orchestra."*

Musin's statement is significant. The development of expressive conducting originates within our soul. *"The art of conducting lay in making music visible with your hands."* This statement quickly triggers a recall to our first conducting classes. The use of hands was insignificant as the class priority was a pattern. Our right hand held the baton while beating a basic pattern and the left hand indicated dynamics and cues. Do the current conditions (classes, clinics, etc.) indicate our weakness to discuss and teach musical expression through natural, spontaneous physical movements? I think so. Perhaps Furtwangler says it best, *"Either you have it or you don't."*

Words: Subtleties of Nuance and Inflection

"The heart of the melody can never be put down on paper."
— Pablo Casals

We have many words that describe artistic thoughts and expression. Simply speaking the words subtlety, nuance, inflection, tension, relief, intensity, soul, and passion, generates the significant value and implications of what we do as musicians. These words also relate to how we feel, how we create and thus express ourselves. How do these words project meaning with our interpretation of literature? It is difficult to describe the word *feeling*. Not until we speak and are deeply aware of the flow and subtle nuance of our speech can we connect with *feeling*. Our day-to-day language is loaded with feeling and meaning. These feelings come from within. Our expression of sadness, joy, or happiness, and with whom we are communicating with at the time, emanates from the core of our innermost feelings. At this stage of my musical career, I am immersed with the emotional connection of speech and music. The emotional impact of speech and music comes from one source within our souls. There is no separation as speech is music and music is speech.

Linking music with our everyday language is the easiest way to become musically expressive. One must recognize the *music* that exists in our speech and reading. The connections are with the rhythmic flow of words and syllables. The inflections of words throughout a sentence create a musical phrase.

Pablo Casal's description of music comes from the depth of his imagination, meaning, and expression. He states, *"We can never exhaust the multiplicity of nuances and subtleties which make the charm of music."* This statement is powerful! Therein lies the secret or mystery of musical expression.

I frequently ask questions throughout my clinics and workshops on how musical expression and feelings are taught. What methods are used to teach such subtle feelings? When I ask the questions, the answer most used is to "tell a story and think about the story or person when playing." The use of imagery is most often a part of teaching expression. In my last publication, I spoke about *exercising expression for meaning.* If we do not exercise expression and only tell *stories*, it will certainly atrophy just as a muscle does from a lack of use.

I have used a speaking exercise in my clinics and workshops to make the connection between expression of words and music. This is the only means I have to make directors aware of *where* musical expression resides and how easily intimidated a person becomes when using spoken expression. This uneasy feeling is simply a result of the sterile, unemotional methods used when teaching conducting. Our voice is a connection to our emotional center, which is the limbic system. The limbic system appears to be primarily responsible for our emotional life, and has a lot to do with the formation of memories.

I find it unusual that we have not considered how to implement *speech expression* and its connection with expressive conducting. We discover a great deal when we listen to people speak with the emotion and inflections that surround their words and sentences. Not only the emotional parts of their words, but the rhythmic flow of words and sentences that embellish meaning and comprehension. As we become excited, determined, sad, or joyous, we immediately project these feelings through our voice. Shouldn't we consider the emotional connections of our speech with how we conduct expressively? Conducting classes fail to implement *speaking exercises*. As long as we continue in this manner, few will ever experience the beauty of musical expression.

When using a speaking exercise, it surely is eye opening when listening to the results. As I ask individuals to read a short statement. I refer to this as being "concert #1". This open-ended learning is free from any right or wrong answers, and focuses simply on expression and creativity from within. Then another individual reads the same statement and that becomes "concert #2". This continues with several renderings of the same statement. I respond to each reading as a "concert." Within a short period, the directors discover what I am doing. The readings become more dramatic, expressive, and at times, explosive. They recognize and make the *emotional connection* with words. Yes, we are responding to the *signs and symbols* of reading (words, commas, periods, exclamation marks). The only differences with the signs and symbols of our language and musical notation are simply in how they are designed and represented. Our emotions come from our limbic system where all types of expression for interpreting signs and symbols originate.

The speaking exercise that I use in my sessions to *break the barriers* of personal expression has been written by notable composer Stephen Melillo. When reading the statement, be sensitive to the pitch variations of words and syllables along with the rhythmic flow. The statement is as follows:

It was a time of turbulence...
When sea-faring men dared claim the waters of the earth...
A time when the crimson blade of treachery,
Slashed across trusting hearts.

Read the statement several times to discover the nuances and flow of words. Think of this as being *music*. Read it again, and you will discover the unlimited variations for personal expression that can be connected to musical phrases.

Now, the challenge! Read the following statement while observing dynamic markings, and tempo indications.

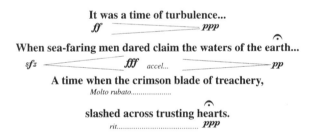

When reading the above statement, I'm sure you felt challenged in attempting to adhere to all the markings. The difference is where the mind is focused. Is it focused on the musical markings or the words? What creates this departure is the mind is consumed with the musical markings and not the phrase statement. The musical markings removed or restricted the natural, expressive flow of the phrase/statement as you experienced in the first readings. This happens with music making. The question is; at what point does the musician or conductor make a musical decision to create an artistic statement? As I stated earlier in this essay, contrived expression is superficial, lacking meaning and depth.

During my sessions, as each director reads the statement above, it is quite apparent how reserved and inhibited they become when trying to be expressive. Unfortunately, the same is true when they play their instruments or conduct. We have difficulty expressing ourselves freely as we are conditioned to expect specific teacher-defined directions for musical expression and correctness. Why is this happening? The largest inhibition we encounter is the fear of risk. It is *risk* that stifles or hinders our expressive potential. Moreover, this is exactly what occurs when musical phrases are played or conducted. The traditional method is to have a teacher dictate where crescendo, decrescendo, accents, etc. should be. This is the extent of conventional methods addressing musical expression. There is a huge gap in our instructional methods dealing with musical expression. To be successful, one needs to be free and expressive with conducting and playing an instrument. If the teacher has not experienced the truth and freedom of musical expression, it will be difficult, if not impossible to teach artistic integrity. As Confucius says, *"How can a caged man teach you to fly"?*

Speaking With Your Hands

Once confidence is established with the above speaking exercise, ask the student to speak the statement while using their hands, arms, and facial expression to enhance/embellish the meaning of the words and statement. The first time they attempt speaking and connecting with their hands, they will feel very clumsy and awkward, which is natural. This speaking exercise with hands and facial expression is extremely important as it immediately establishes a natural *connection* between felt-expression with the mind, hands, arms, face, and passion.

I'm sure that many have observed people that speak with their hands. Not only are their hands a part of active expression, their body language becomes quite animated. This type of expression is very natural for these individuals. It's been said that if you restrict that person's hands, they would not be able to speak. Speaking with your hands is, without question, a significant force for complimenting conducting techniques. Why? Every physical movement is tied or connected to the emotional center of the individual. This is a natural part of expression that compliments conducting.

The voice utterance and physical movements connect the nuance and inflection with the energy of thought and felt expression. Once comfort is established, the hand moves only need to be shaped to convey poise, finesse, deliberateness, power, and gentleness, to name a few descriptors. A comparison can be made with a ballet dancer as their hands project the sensitive motion, poise, and finesse shaped by their physical movements and inner feelings.

If music expresses emotion spontaneously, shouldn't all our conducting moves be spontaneous relative to the style of the music? So many publications, clinics, workshops, and symposiums document specific *moves or patterns* for every musical inflection or nuance. Rather than being encumbered with such programmed moves, and consuming the hours to learn such patterns, I believe it is much easier to create a personal, unique *vocabulary* of spontaneous moves. This is obvious when viewing the most notable conductors of our premier symphony orchestras. There are no two alike. Each has his or her personal, intimate, and innate conducting presence.

H. Robert Reynolds believes we should have a great variety of gestures, but conducting technique really comes from inside the person. He goes on further stating, *"I cannot give somebody my conducting technique because they are a different person. This is much like the way we use hand gestures while talking, but it helps to have a wide array of hand gestures while talking or conducting. Gestures have to come from within, not because they were learned. The basics of grammar can be learned; the ability to communicate comes from within."*

The Final Test:
Developing Poise and Finesse with Conducting

We now approach the final "musical awareness" test! Return to the first few times you read **"It was a time of turbulence"** statement and silently "express" the words with your hands. *This makes the "conducting connection" with your silent thoughts (musical).* The flow of musical thought is now projected through your arms, hands, and facial expression creating meaningful gestures. The barriers that restricted conducting movements are removed.

This exercise is, without doubt, the most important exercise you will ever experience when training to become a conductor. We have been so conditioned to pattern movement with our arms. Any departure from such patterns creates clumsy and awkward movements. The critical purpose for this type of free form movement is to develop poise. Flowing, and unobtrusive movements best create the flow and beauty of musical expression.

Speaking exercises through dramatic expression provides the shortest avenue to the truth and integrity of musical expression. This opens the doors to create *meaning* with our hands, face, and physical movements that connect to the conductor's passion of inner feelings (soul). The result is musical truth and integrity, and not something contrived, prescribed, or imitated.

Natural Laws of
Musical Expression

I believe that many methods and rehearsal techniques fail to go beyond the crescendo and decrescendo descriptions with phrasing. The thoughtful flow of musical energy and musical phrases move in and out of silence with forward direction through passionate and expressive guidance. Igor Stravinsky makes a powerful statement that prompts thoughtful musical energy. He states, *"All music is nothing more than a succession of impulses that converge towards a definite point of repose."* Such statements, along with many others that I discovered through reading and research, prompted my design of the *Natural Laws of Musical Expression*. After reading the many publications that address the complexities of expression, I realized the methods were directed to the technique of conducting with little attention to musical expression. There seemed to be a fear of addressing the emotion and feeling of a musical phrase.

After many years of conducting and performance, I arrived at three simple concepts that energize melodic, harmonic, and rhythm patterns. I frequently speak about these natural laws in my previous publications.

The three four-word concepts are:

1. Short searches for long
2. Low searches for high
3. High searches for low

The word *"searches"* implies energy, motion, and forward movement looking for a point of repose. *Short searches for long. Long* is the arrival note or *point of repose/relief. Low searches for high. High* is the *point of repose/relief. High searches for low. Low* is the *point of repose/relief.*

When applying this concept to phrases, determine the low and high note in the phrase. The notes between create the feeling of energy and motion moving to the high note. The notes between create the *tension.* The arrival of the high note is the *relief* of the phrase or point of repose. Robert Shaw stated, *"A phrase is departing from, passing through, and arriving at"* to create musical meaning. Applying this statement to *low searching for high* simply means departing from the low note, passing through the notes between and arriving at the high note. When a phrase is perceived in this manner, subtle nuances and inflections enhance the artistic interpretation. This energy of thought must *point to something*, creating forward motion/ energy, intensity, and direction. It is inherent that thoughtful energy energizes musical movement, thus, shaping the direction of a phrase from beginning to end.

On the following page is an illustration of the three concepts; *High searches for Low, Low searches for High*, and *Short searches for Long.* As the graphic illustrates, the arrow is pointing to the *relief* or *point of repose*. I also included beat 4 moving to 5. Why? As you count from 4 to 5, listen carefully to the *arrival* of 5. Your voice has a downward sound when saying 5. This subtlety indicates the *feeling* of arriving or acknowledging the arrival, the energy of musical thought!

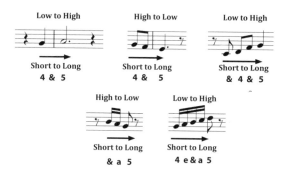

The following illustrates the three concepts placed on Percy Grainger's *Irish Tune.* The concepts open up countless subtle nuances and inflections that are unique to each musician and conductor (as no two can be alike). I did place the *beats* below the melody only to attempt to describe possibilities for interpretation by referring to the beat.

- 1st measure leading to the 2nd measure ... beats 2, 3, & 4 point to the dotted half note (H). Consider moving from beat 2 with slight intensity moving to beat 3 and slight length on beat 4 to create anticipation/tension before the arrival of beat 1 (H).
- 2nd measure, on beat 4 ... begin "searching for beat 2 (H) in the 3rd measure ... beat 2 of the 3rd measure begins searching for beat 3 and 4 (L) of the 4th measure
- beat 2 in 5th measure begins searching for beat 1 (H) of measure 6.
- All the indicators for short (S) searching for long (L) should have a slight feeling of tension and length before relief that follows.

Other Examples

As you will quickly discover, your performing and conducting will become very expressive simply by creating this *thoughtful musical energy* of forward movement as indicated in the above examples. Moreover, when attending concerts the difference between the truth of musical expression and the prescription of sterile performance will be quite apparent. I can assure you with these concepts in place, you will add another dimension to your musical skills and conducting.

Many of the current texts describing musical expression fail to acknowledge these underlying principles and the importance of the thought process that triggers the movement of an expressive melodic line. Many attempts have been made to create this in forms of markings, brackets, dynamics, or other symbols that have very little to do with the spontaneity and integrity of producing an expressive phrase. Consider our everyday speech. Do we consider the length of vowels, syllables as we speak? If we do what we do with music, our speech would not be understandable. As David Levitin writes, *"So much of the research on musical expertise has looked for accomplishment in the wrong place, in the facility of fingers rather than the expressiveness of emotion.*

Expressing Music
through Gesture

"It has been said that there are two kinds of conductors: those who handle traffic and those who make music."

— FRANK BATTISTI

Expressing music through gesture determines the success of a conductor. Many of our conducting symposiums and workshops frequently address the art of mime. Mime is a wonderful means to address the beauty and flow of artistic expression through body language. The connections between conducting and mime are significant as we consider phrasing, clarity, pacing, style, articulation, and dynamics. The gestures made by mimes are driven by the same intentions of a conductor. As conductors, we are consumed with the clarity of our gestures for efficiency.

Another avenue that significantly improves conducting is what I refer to as free-form conducting. Such movements are important when developing a unique sense of musical interpretation. Free-form movement helps the conductor communicate meaning and goes beyond the unmusical or visual distractions of conducting patterns. Much like mime. By not using the standard 2-, 3-, or 4-beat conducting patterns, this free, improvised movement releases the constraints that inhibit the more expressive and natural movement of the arms, wrists, palms, and fingers. Free-form conducting may include long flowing circles and lines shaped with arms, wrists, and hands in musically inspired motion, feeling, and expression. Such movement projects the inner grace, flow, and poise within a musical phrase or composition. The movements are similar to the graceful motions and elegant lines of a ballerina moving through space.

Erich Leinsdorf states that, *"Gestures are born out of the need that arises only during music making. They cannot be determined in advance."* Frank Battisti stated that *"there are three ways a conductor can communicate to players: through representative gestures, expressive mime gestures, and explanation by word of mouth. Representative gestures are conservative, disciplined, and un-decorative; expressive mime gestures are freer and include varying degrees of pantomime. Of course, communication by word of mouth is obvious."*

The exercises that follow enhance and embellish conducting movements with meaning; they develop poise and provide opportunities to articulate internal expressive interpretation more efficiently. Similar to mime, these exercises are a form of body language. Such exercises create an important connection with our feelings and our physical expression, bringing us close to the goal of making musical meaning. A word of warning: if not immersed in the flow of music (phrases and so on), the exercises will be meaningless. The intent is to elevate our musical awareness with the subtleties and energy of melodic lyricism.

Free-form conducting is simply improvisation of a conductor's physical movements prompted by the flow of music. It is a natural connection to *speaking with your hands* and the *speaking exercise* introduced earlier in this document. This process connects spontaneously to rhythm, pitch, tone, and dynamics without reading notation. Dalcroze stated, *"Gesture must define musical emotion and call up its image. Gesture itself is nothing—its whole value depends on the emotion that inspires it."*

Exercising Musical Gestures

To begin, select a recording of an unknown chorale, ballad, folk song, or other similar composition in an adagio tempo. Listen carefully to the flow of music. As the selection plays, make long flowing movements with arms and hands. Do not use a baton or follow any previously learned conducting pattern. While you are listening, don't consume thoughts to any type of analytical (rhythm, melody, etc.) detail. Focus your attention to the flow of phrases, energy, tension and relief, softness, lightness, bold, aggressive, or gentle characteristics of the music. Try to flow with the phrases and motion of the music without any type of conducting form!

Removing the familiar conducting patterns requires making expressive movements with arms, hands, and facial expression. A natural reaction to this exercise is feeling clumsy. The goal is to have your movements reflect a spontaneous reaction to the subtleties of nuance and inflection. Do this frequently and you will gain a considerable amount of freedom with your arms and hands. Such an exercise demands and develops a closer connection with our feelings and soul, and brings us closer to authentic expression. This technique is similar to *mime*. It is a means of expression through body language.

1. Start from a center position with hands and arms slightly extended forward inside shoulder and eye level.

2. Make your movements with long, circular lines and shapes projecting grace, poise, and freedom with hands, fingers, and wrists. Do not use 2, 3, or 4 beat patterns.

3. As the music continues, focus your movements and facial expression to the following:
   - *Touch and feel the space before you . . . the space of silence! . . .*
   - *Expand and contract the space of silence with your hands . . .*
   - *Make all movements connected, smooth, flowing . . .*
   - *Realize that hand/finger motions are enhanced with facial expressions . . .*

- *Roll, in a circular motion as the music unfolds and expands . . .*
- *Feel the space between the long lines . . . touch the space . . .*
- *Speak silently through the movements of the left hand . . .*
- *Speak silently through the movements of the right hand . . .*
- *Feel the difference between left and right hand . . .*
- *Appeal to the imagined ensemble for more expression . . .*
- *Neglect beat or pulse tempo.. It 'lives' within the music . . .*
- *Sense and 'feel the time that lives' within the music . . .*
- *Float over and on top of the music and sound . . . soaring . . .*

4. Select a recording of a march. As the march continues, focus your movements and facial expressions to the following:
    - *Flowing lines, implying the energy of March style . . .*
    - *Shaping phrases with hands and fingers . . .*
    - *Avoiding patterns or movements that imply pulse or tempo . . .*
    - *Emphasizing slight nuances with fingers and hand movements . . .*
    - *Creating more abrupt moves where music dictates . . .*
    - *Incorporating firm facial reaction expressing the dignity of a march . . .*
    - *Moving to a center position . . . imply time with slight finger movement (Bourgeois Style, former Conductor of the US Marine Band)*

5. Expand the free form improvisational conducting exercises to other styles of literature. As you gain freedom in both thought and physical movement, your conducting will convey sensitivity to feeling and expression. The line shapes and motions you create release a style of communication through your body language. If such movements are not prompted from the beauty and passion within your mind, the long flowing lines of music will appear to be meaningless and foolish. This process is an avenue for making a mind/body connection with thoughtful feeling guided by the beauty of musical phrases.

Another important consideration should be given to horizontal conducting movements versus vertical patterns. There is a huge difference between these two approaches. Throughout my adjudicating travels, I often commented to bands that they needed to have more lyricism and flow within the literature they programmed. Frequently, the phrases were abrupt and projected more attention to note and rhythm patterns rather than the direction of a phrase. To help eliminate this type of note-by-note performance, I often suggested consideration be given to more horizontal flow with conducting gestures. The horizontal movement is connected to the forward flow and direction of a phrase. Horizontal movement is opposite to the more vertical conducting patterns such as 4/4, 3/4, or 2/4 time signatures. Please don't misunderstand; I realize the need for these conducting patterns. But, what I am suggesting is moving from the rigidity of patterns to a more lyrical flowing pattern. Visually, the musicians' response immediately changes as such movements prompt a lyrical energy of thought.

Gradually start using these motions when conducting your ensemble. When you gain freedom in your conducting techniques, and start perceiving and implying the motion and flow of phrases, the students will react to the visual nature and styles of your conducting patterns and make beautiful music! A word of caution is appropriate regarding your conducting gestures. Most important is that your movements not be excessive. It is easy to encourage loud and unbalanced playing through extreme movements.

PART II

Interpretation: Looking Beyond Notation

"However accurately a music piece may be written, however carefully all possible ambiguities may be excluded — by indicating tempos, colors, timbres, etc., — it will always contain hidden elements which escape us, because the dialectic of language is unable to define music's dialectic in its entirety. Thus, the realization of these hidden elements is a matter of experience and insight. In other words, it is a matter of the talent of the man who is evoked to play the music."

—*MUSICAL POETICS*, IGOR STRAVINSKY

Interpretation has many meanings when conducting. It is the conductor's distinctive personal version of a piece of music based on his or her knowledge and extensive performance experience. Unrelenting creative expression shapes harmony, melody, and rhythm, identifying "your" inter-pretation. It is your uniqueness that makes the difference while exceeding the restrictions of notation.

We have "rules" of interpretation, or, "respecting the composer's intentions." If rules are in place, why then do our "authorities of interpretation" performances sound nothing like one another? What happens to interpretation when a composer conducts his own music? What are the "traditions" of interpretation and do you consider these traditions as copies or imitations? These are just a few of the questions that trigger a search of what and why interpretation is so important when conducting an ensemble.

We have many bands that are what I refer to as "sound-a-like." Everything is preprogrammed and has nothing to do with Music. I find this objectionable when speaking and dealing with the "art of music." Expression and tempo are subject to interpretation. It cannot be any other way. When I refer to "sound-a-like" bands, it is obvious all musical details have been "programmed."

As an adjudicator, we have heard many bands that "play the exercise." This is a troubling situation. I'm not sure this will ever change. My only hope is that with all the conducting symposiums, workshops, and clinic presentations we have in place, that musical expression will be rightly taught. Currently, more time is spent on the "mechanics" of conducting with less attention to expressivity.

I found it quite interesting to read, *Interpretation of Music*, by Thurston Dart who stated, *"Interpretation means a restoration of musical conventions for the most part long obsolete and forgotten."* Moreover, Laurence Dreyfus, in his essay, "Beyond Interpretation of Music," states, *"We fight about how music should be played because we assert competing sets of values, and defend them by applying 'rules' of interpretation according to different criteria. Such is the case with 'respecting the composer's intentions', an interpretive rule — or is it a mantra? — which few musicians dare to flout, but which authorizes performance which sound nothing like one another."* Dreyfus goes on further to speak about the 'authorities' such as, *"(1) performers' traditions, as in the assertion that this is the way we have always done it; (2) musicological rectitude; (3) musical structure (as defined by music theorists and analysts); and (4) musical common sense. These authorities validate interpretations, to assure us that we are doing the right thing, and to help pass on interpretive practices (or copies) to the next generation."*

I share two most notable quotes regarding interpretation by Leopold Auer, great violin pedagogue of the early twentieth century who taught Mischa Elman, Jascha Heifetz, and Pablo Casals. Leopold Auer stated, *"One tradition only do I recognize- that it is the function of the artist to enter in the spirit of a composition, and reveal to us the intentions of the composer. The musical message of the composer, the true spirit of his inspiration, the soul of his music–that is what we are interested in. Though no two great artists now playing before the public interpret the Bach Chaconne, in exactly the same manner. The artist of today will play Bach as he should be played, and will play Bach better because he will play him in the interpretative spirit of our own generation, not that of 1720."*

Pablo Casals stated, *"The performer, looking at the score in front of him has got to reconstitute, not a so-called objectivity, but all the different phases which the composer's mind went through when creating this work, and in doing so, observe the reactions which they produce deep down in his own mind. There are so many excellent instrumentalists who are completely obsessed by the printed note, whereas it has a very limited power to express what the music actually means. Are there any sets of rules for this re-creating process? I cannot think of any."*

Notable conductor Herbert Blomstedt states, *"Music is revelation! It must say something, it must tell a truth that is human or divine or both. Just delivering notes, even if it's perfect, doesn't give this revelation at all. Performance is a personal witness; it is the way the conductor sees its meaning or message. It is in his mind, and he has caught a glimpse of the composer's vision and gives it just as personally as if the composer would conduct it."*

H. Robert Reynolds had this to say about interpretation, *"I hope this doesn't shock you too much, but in my view, much of what has been written about how to think about interpreting music is misconceived. We should think as little as possible. We should think as much as necessary but as little as possible because thought very often gets in the way of artistic sense."* He goes on further to state, *"Take the chance of being reprimanded with your interpretation, but in doing so, give your soul to the music."*

We have many opportunities through symposiums, clinics, and workshops that can easily lead us into copying or imitating interpretation. Imitation simply never projects the integrity of a conductor's unique musical imagination. Too often, through musical analysis procedures, interpretation becomes a computer/mathematical like result. When analyzing a composition, it is very easy to miss the composer's intent or the "whole" of the composition by focusing too much on the smaller fragments of notation. The subtle nuances and inflections that surround the melody, rhythm, and harmony created by the conductor and musicians evolve meaning and appreciation. These, coupled with transitions and modulations, are all we have to work with when designing the interpretation of a composition. What is most important is in how we perceive the "whole" of the composition. I discovered a statement written by German Poet, Friedrich Holderlin. He stated, " *If man does not find the time for looking at the whole he will stumble again and again. He can only see small things without any context.*" He further states, *"Man must learn to see things as a whole. Then everything will be good and beautiful!* (From, *"The Drama of Modern Mankind—according to thoughts of Friedrich Hölderlin")*.

The artistic considerations for musical expression are impossible to notate. Our decisions are based on things that are unknown and intangible. We so often see and hear the attempts to prescribe expression through the use of various markings. However, expression lies within every individual as distinct and dynamic entities, just as fingerprints are solely unique to every individual. As a professional clarinetist, I am convinced that for a musician to be expressive requires a thought process totally consumed with the sound being produced and not the signs and symbols surrounding notation. Countless publications currently address musical expression, and, musical expression continues to remain a mystery. Without musical expression, interpretation is non-existent.

Frequently we speak of correct and incorrect interpretations. What may be considered to be an incorrect interpretation may be justifiable to the conductor based on their knowledge and conducting experiences. Too often, a questionable interpretation encompasses incorrect tempo, stifling and restrictive responses to phrasing and dynamics, and little regard for style or expressivity.

It is most annoying to attend a concert and hear a "note perfect" performance void of expression. Do we consider this to be correct interpretation? Unfortunately, the signs and symbols have no meaning until the musicians and conductor bring them to "life". When teaching musical expression I often state, *"notes remain trivial until they are animated by feeling and spirit."*

Through my years of teaching and adjudicating, the most profound problem I observe is that directors fail to do their "musical homework" when it comes to designing their performance of a major composition. In fact, one of the most disturbing performances I heard as an adjudicator was the Holst, *Fantasia on a Dargason*. The movement was played in a slow six beat tempo. Yes, very difficult to listen to. I do believe this director failed to research the composition.

The misconceptions and discrepancies that continue to occur with interpretation, musical expression, and phrasing are due to inconsistent preparation by the instrumental teacher. University classes should be devoted to the study of all wind masterworks. Such a class would provide every future director the opportunity to conduct most of the masterworks throughout a four-year program. This surely would solve many of the musical problems that exist with our young directors. In my opinion though, if the person teaching this course is consumed only with notation and is a "note perfect" conductor, this type of class won't necessarily support expression and interpretation.

CHAPTER

9

Creating Meaning

"Technique is not music. . . . Music is the thousandth of a millisecond between one note and another, how you get from one to the other—that's where the music is."

—ISAAC STERN

A conductor's distinctive personal interpretation is what makes a composition unique from all others. As musicians and conductors, we are immersed in the fine art of detail, encompassing a multitude of subtle embellishments that are impossible to notate and extremely difficult to teach. We must acknowledge the significant statement made by Pablo Casals: *"We can never exhaust the multiplicity of nuances and subtleties which make the charm of music. . . . We tend to be inhibited by the printed score with its scarcity of expressive markings."* Such nuances are impossible to define. I believe it takes many years for a musician or conductor to recognize these finite musical details because such musical subtleties are not presented or taught in our preparation as a band director.

Each conductor has his or her own interpretive ideas. Interpretation is unique with every musician. The differences are much like our taste buds. I like chocolate ice cream and you like vanilla, or, I like beef and you like seafood. No two people hear the same thing nor do they see the same things in a painting. What are the differences between conductors? There is only one difference and that is how each perceives music. Their perception of music dictates their performance, conducting, and literature selection.

If I conduct a composition several times, each time is different. I do not believe that artistic interpretation can be the same each time a selection is performed. If this happens, it no longer exists as artistic expression. To teach artistry requires a teacher who understands the spontaneity of artistic expression. It is easy to be consumed with the written notation. As Pablo Casals states, *"There are so many excellent instrumentalists who are completely obsessed by the printed note, whereas it has a very limited power to express what the music actually means."* The uniqueness of interpretation is determined by how we deal with the unadorned markings of musical notation to create meaning and value.

I often use the analogy of a Rembrandt painting with a musical performance. I stated earlier that artistic interpretation couldn't be the same each time. If so, it no longer exists as artistic expression. Consider a Rembrandt painting and what the result would be if he decided to re-paint the picture. Would it be identical? Could all the subtleties of color inflections and nuances be repeated?

Musical intelligence plays an important role when interpreting a score. Musical intelligence is having the ability to *"read between the lines and beyond the boundaries of notation,"* where artistic considerations and expression are found. Musical intelligence is the result of years of study, practice, and listening with intense focus on the smallest details in search of perfection. As conductors, we must have the ability to look beyond the printed notes.

Ultimately, the ensemble will naturally sense the feeling a conductor has within his or her mind and soul. It is this energy of thoughtful expression that is given to the players. Musicians can sense this connection immediately and respond accordingly. If it becomes imitated or contrived, the conductor is a detriment to the ensemble's music-making potential.

Artistic Considerations

"The pedagogy of conducting has focused on the teaching of technique. The stuff that allows the creation of great music is rarely dealt with in the teaching of conducting."

—JAMES JORDAN

I frequently refer to the energy of musical thinking as "artistic thought" or "artistic considerations." These terms play a significant role in developing an "artistic vocabulary". When implemented within a performance, these ideas clearly distinguish a superior conductor from an average conductor. If artistic thought has not been exercised, how can one believe that the musical result will be artistic?

Artistic considerations are determined by the conductor's artistic vocabulary, which are beyond the unadorned markings of musical notation. Artistic considerations are the "secrets" of recognized master performers, conductors, and teachers. A few of the most influential publications I found that address artistic thought are, David Blum's *Casals and the Art of Interpretation*, James Jordan's *A Musician's Soul*, John Krell's *Kincaidiana*, and Donald Barra's *Dynamic Performance*, and Eugene Migliaro Corporan's Chapters found in the seven GIA volumes of *Teaching Music Through Performance in Band*,

Throughout my guest conducting, I use four statements when teaching musical artistry. The concepts enhance artistic considerations and musical decisions. The first is, (1) *"Music is sound moving in and out of silence."* This statement plays a significant role in how music is perceived and dissolves the boundaries of notation. Music is an art, but too often, becomes a "paint by number" exercise with the fear of going outside the boundaries of notation (as in preparing for an adjudication and not daring to go beyond the unadorned musical notation). I teach students to imagine an artist's brush "lifting off into the white of canvas," the sound disappears into infinity or the white of the canvas, dissolving the boundaries of notation.

Applying this statement to musical sound and allowing our "canvas" to be "silence," we discover the "right side" of a note as we "lift the sound off into silence" without a contrived end, simply decaying into silence.

The next statement is, (2) *"Don't play square notes."* The meaning of this statement is simple; "Square notes" lack personality and are uncharacteristic to the style of music being performed. It is connected to *"music is sound moving in and out of silence."* All notes must have "life" and are energized with nuance and inflection. Moreover, square notes are much like "painting by number" and not going outside the boundary lines. Consider the natural decay of a note beyond the boundary line. The subtle musical nuances and inflections are impossible to notate, and are left up to the player and conductor to interpret. Playing notes and rhythms precisely as they appear produces sterile and uncharacteristic sounds with no meaning attached.

The third statement is, (3) *"Notes remain trivial until they are animated with feeling and spirit."* This statement is connected to the first two statements about sound into silence and square notes. I am simply making the case for music having personality and character. Music is alive and must "say something"! It is an extension of my favorite quote by Pablo Casals, *"We can never exhaust the multiplicity of nuances and subtleties which make the charm of music."* My teacher always told me that musical expression is found behind the notes. There is nothing behind the notes, only you. Your musical imagination, personality, and expressivity create and embellish the charm of music. This is what makes music unique with every musician and conductor.

The last statement is, (4) *"If you can't say it, you can't play it."* This not only holds true for phrasing and expression, but also for rhythmic articulation. Students misunderstand rhythm patterns because they were never required to speak them. I taught my students to speak the rhythm pattern with subdivided patterns. Simply stated, *"If you can't say it, you can't play it."* If you can't say it, it's obvious you don't understand it. "Rhythmic intelligence" must be projected through the instrument. The instrument has no intelligence.

These four statements are powerful insights essential to ensembles. Don't let the simplicity of these statements fool you. They hold considerable musical depth and meaning.

I have no fears to be free with my interpretation. My musical decisions are based on my "reservoir of artistic considerations" that evolved from more than fifty years as a professional musician and educator. Artistic considerations evolve within our inner feelings and identify our uniqueness. This is where my decisions come from when I consider my interpretation of a composition. A few of my decisions come from the following:

1. Dynamic levels, either less or more from what is indicated as I shape ensemble sonority;
2. Slight retards or suspensions where melodic and harmonic content dictate;
3. Increasing the energy and intensity of a phrase to its point of repose;
4. Metronome markings. If I feel the tempo indicated is too slow or too fast to capture the style that "I" believe the composer intended;
5. Ritards when arriving at a transition or key change to create anticipation;
6. Slight fermatas where appropriate harmonically; or
7. Slightly exaggerating or lengthening a note or notes within a phrase or rhythm pattern to create more anticipation before the point of repose.

These are only a few of the musical liberties I use when conducting. They cannot be notated, as they occur spontaneously. What is important is the spontaneity that can only come from the conductor being immersed in what the composer has created.

As I conduct, my interpretation is based on listening vertically for harmonic content and coupling this with the musical decisions I make with the melodic horizontal line. These harmonic and melodic decisions are made through what I refer to as the "three natural laws of expression" of which I presented earlier in this publication.

Enhancing the Depth of Listening

We have spent many years attempting to categorize, collect, and document "specifics" that will assist directors when dealing with interpretation. Can we define the multiplicity of nuances and subtleties of which Casals speaks about? Such decisions are only based on the musicianship of the conductor or musician. Our "liking" must be based on a solid musical foundation and not something random or reckless that will distort the composer's intent. This musical foundation is the difference between poor, average, and superior performance.

I often listen to recordings by Frederick Fennell, Harry Begian, Donald Hunsberger, Frank Battisti, H. Robert Reynolds, John Paynter, Col. John Bourgeois, and Col. Arnald Gabriel, to name a few. I believe listening to recordings should be a high priority. It is the only way, other than live performances, to hear the uniqueness and individuality of the musicianship by such notable conductors. This is our avenue to discover and develop the smallest musical entity that makes the charm of musical expression. Moreover, it is the best means to enhance and expand our "reservoir of artistic considerations" as we mature as conductors.

Many individuals do not support listening to recordings while studying literature. I disagree wholeheartedly with such suggestions. We develop an appreciation and understanding for artistic creations by seeing and hearing music, paintings, sculpture, ballet, opera, and other art forms. Artistry is complimented significantly by what we hear, see, and touch. Such experiences shape the meaning of beauty within our mind and soul.

I compare this to the natural learning process. We first learned to speak by listening to the "word" before learning to spell and write the "word." As a child, if you didn't hear the word first, the word did not become a part of your growing vocabulary. We can pronounce a word a thousand different ways by simply changing the nuance and inflections that we have "stored" in our memory banks. Hearing is the first critical issue that determines our vocabulary. Hearing also provides an avenue to our musical performance vocabulary. We encourage students to listen to notable soloists to develop a concept of tone. I strongly support listening to recordings, live concerts, soloists, and every form of music to broaden our musical perceptions. This simply compliments our musical interpretation and expression. I often heard the statement that we must first establish our own interpretation before listening to a recording. This is rather difficult to do if an individual has no "musical reserve" in place to draw from past musical experiences.

My interpretation of a composition evolves through my score study. I believe there is a "line or gap" separating an artistic performance from a preplanned performance. What determines an artistic interpretation? How are artistic decisions made and are they relevant for musical meaning to occur? These are essential questions to consider. I believe artistic performance is spontaneous and not programmed. As musicians and conductors we are immersed in the fine art of detail. This encompasses a multitude of subtle embellishments that are impossible to notate and extremely difficult to teach. To teach artistry requires a director who understands and is able to demonstrate the spontaneity of artistic expression and not something contrived. This Chinese proverb says it all, *"How can a caged man teach you to fly?"* If one is not musically expressive as an instrumentalist or conductor, one is not able to understand or teach artistic expression (*the caged man*).

PART III

Emotions and Music Making

"You must give each note life, your life.

You must sacrifice . . .

You must learn to give yourself to music . . .

Then you will make it live . . .

Then you will be able to make other people understand music."

— NADIA BOULANGER

A topic that is very seldom addressed in our profession deals with the emotions of music making. Perhaps this topic has not received the attention necessary because of its vagueness and depth. Emotions are an extremely important element within the entirety of a musical performance. It is our emotional response that shapes the beauty and expressive qualities of our interpretation and conducting. This is the uniqueness between individuals and conductors. Our emotions are the result of our life and musical experiences.

Emotions are based on our beliefs, actions, intentions, and interpretations. Emotions exert an incredibly powerful force on human behavior and our music making experiences. In psychology, emotion is often defined as a complex state of feeling that results in physical and psychological changes that influence thought and behavior. Emotionality is associated with a range of psychological phenomena including temperament, personality, mood, and motivation.

Emotions play a significant role with our interpretation of literature. Consider the emotional thought process required to create expressive phrasing, styles, sonority, and transitions. When guest conducting, I am totally aware of my emotional involvement to create the intensity, beauty, and expressive elements necessary for the "unforgettable musical performance." As Pablo Casals states, *"The heart of the melody can never be put down on paper."* It is our soul and passion that must be immersed in the energy of musical thought and body language.

Emotion must surround interpretation. If not, music is missing an intimate connection with the soul of the conductor. Musicians and audience easily detect the lack of emotion. This is the difference in a superior, mediocre, or poor musical performance and represents the depth of musicianship.

Conductor Carl St. Clair of the Pacific Symphony Orchestra states, *"Until you appeal to the students' personal mind, they are doing exactly what you are conducting ... things that are not innately expressive ... things that are together, in rhythm, in time. It won't be a note of music until they start playing from their natural expressive emotional center ... releasing without fear, their feeling."*

The emotional response to beauty, compassion, appreciation, self-esteem, cooperation, and respect are but a few "living" priorities that are hidden in music study and performance. Our values are determined by our knowledge base. If our depth of understanding is shallow, the values we hold for musical excellence will be shallow. Musical decisions are based on what we know and understand. Donald Barra states, *"Harmony provides a tonal skeleton against which melodies develop, and it also creates a pattern of motion that contains its own sequence of thrusts and resolutions. "*

It is quite obvious that there are many programs that perceive music as simply a response to musical notation. If this happens, the "heart" and emotion of interpretation, phrasing, and expression will never surface. This type of understanding represents those who never experienced the beauty and soul of musical language. It is simply an exercise and nothing more.

Tension and the Point of Repose

"All music is nothing more than a succession of impulses that converge towards a definite point of repose"

—IGOR STRAVINSKY

Interpretation, phrasing, emotion, tension, and relief are based on melodic, harmonic, and rhythmic content. These are significant factors determining the artistic quality of a musical performance. Conductor, author, Donald Barra has this to say in his publication, *The Dynamic Performance... "Feeling arises from our inhibited or suppressed desires and expectations. This inhibited energy, or tension, forms the basis of our emotional response. "*(page 28) He goes on further to say, *"It is not the development of tension, but the prolongation of tension, that is the basis of our deeply felt emotional experience. "* (page 29)

Notable composer, Stephen Melillo states, *"Any tension can be resolved to ANY place. Tension is any moment where dissonance takes place."* Musical and emotional decisions are determined by the tension created harmonically with its resolution as the point of repose. Chord qualities create tension and relief. As an example, a dominant chord is relieved by a tonic chord and a bIIm7 is relieved by a tonic are examples of harmonic tension to relief. Other examples are augmented chords, diminished chords, and dissonances.

What dictates tension and relief? We have been taught to analyze compositions to discover "meaning." I strongly believe, as a conductor, one must listen and experience the "feel of music". When does it feel *tense* and when does it feel *still* and resolved? As composer Stephen Melillo further states, *"Analysis leaves one paralyzed...we must forgo "analysis" and simply FEEL and simply LISTEN to music...it is natural."* Analysis simply directs focus and attention to the "bits and pieces" of a musical composition. Don't misunderstand as to what I am saying, analysis is important, but not to a point where we lose sight of the composition as a whole.

The expressive potential of any piece depends upon the nature of its harmonic structure, the shape of its rhythmic patterns, the quality of its melodic growth, and the dynamic character of its tonal relationships. Musical expression is enhanced through the subtleties of nuance and inflection surrounding the notes of a phrase for meaning, value, and understanding. The elusive "life" of each note rests in its progression from its beginning, *through* its duration, and how it terminates or joins to the note that follows. Notable musician and teacher Marcel Tabuteau states, *"I have always been in favor to play as I think. Of course, the ideal combination would be to play with thinking and intelligent feeling. If you think beautifully, you play beautifully."*

In addition to my *Natural Laws of Musical Expression*, I often refer to Robert Shaw's description of a melody. He states, *"Melody, as an abstraction, lies in the amount of tension or relaxation passed by each note to its successor (or received from its predecessor) until the musical sentence is complete and the moment or rest occurs."* He goes on further to say, *"There are three postures of melodic energy; (1) departing from... (2) passing through... (3) arriving at..."*

David McGill, bassoonist with the Chicago Symphony states, *"Phrasing is the crucial element of life the performer adds to the music. A kaleidoscopic variety of colors, intensities, and inflections that holds the interest of the listener and highlights the composer's message."* He further states, *"The spoken line is the template for the musical line. The shape of the spoken line is a smooth progression toward an important word, an arrival at the point of the statement."*

Emotion is a critical ingredient in the art of musical expression. It consumes every moment of our life through speaking, reading, writing, physical activity, and making music. It is reflected through our musical personality as we shape the artistic elements of composers such as Mozart,

Brahms, Williams, Chance, Bach, Holst, Vaughan Williams, Grainger, Beethoven, Milhaud, Stravinsky, and Mahler. The level of emotional involvement when conducting is not the same with all conductors.

As conductors, we are responsible to guide everyone to perceive the musical expectation together, as one person, and not varied individuals throughout the group. Donald Barra writes in his well-known publication, *The Dynamic Performance*, *"The personality of the conductor/performer will influence the character of his/her performance. Past experiences and attitudes will affect the view of this expressive balance."*

"By virtue of our innate intelligence and human capacity to express and feel our emotions, we are all born with the potential to be musically expressive ... the levels can be raised with proper guidance. Depth of expression is not a talent. The real talent that leads to musical expression is intelligence ... the development of expression is the development of the intellect."...David McGill, Chicago Symphony

The Mystery is Solved

As we arrive at this point in this publication, it is my hope that your perception for the art of musical performance has been expanded into a new dimension. As you read through the previous chapters, you experienced music and conducting in a different setting from many conventional methods that have been in use for so many years. Looking outside the **window** of tradition and convention, we see things never before possible. Inside this huge **room**, we see things that were invisible and seldom addressed; the natural flow of phrasing, the subtle inflections of rhythm patterns, the various colors, and layers of dynamics and choirs, unique personal nuances, and inflections, tension, points of repose, are but a few of the **mysteries** we have been trying to discover for so many years.

My system of musical learning addresses the depth of musical performance and conducting for your consideration. It is impossible to speak about artistry if we have not seen or heard artistic expression (how can a caged man teach you to fly). Our perception of music is expanded considerably, and the boundaries of notation disappear exposing the **mystery of music**. The depth and meaning for music are elevated into a new **mind** and **soul** surrounded by passion. Artistic considerations are free to shape your performance for meaningful appreciation and value. The sterile, analytical approach to the art of music has disappeared.

Questions will arise, and fear will be apparent. These are normal reactions as you are experiencing a new setting for something never before considered. Throughout our many years of study, practice, and performance, we **made** music happen. Making music happen is an unnatural occurrence. Making music happen creates too many problems that are often left unresolved.

The natural approach to music is to **allow** it to happen. We cannot impose things that have nothing to do with musical expression. If we feel and listen to the intensity of music and its motion, then the result is what music was intended to be. We are free to indulge in music's beauty of sound and expression. Allowing music to happen becomes a spontaneous occurrence and not contrived or **fixed** to be something that is not natural.

Finale

My intention with this text was to create a deeper awareness of *what* exists in the thought process and mind of a conductor creating artistic musical expression. The areas that were presented evolve from our emotional musical center creating a physical and visual representation for expressive conducting. It is difficult to manifest our innermost passion and feelings, and perhaps this is one reason why musical expression is not a part of our training. It takes deep thought to arrive at an awareness and sensitivity about what we, as conductors, are actually thinking while immersed in our musical performance. It was my intention to present these thoughts, concepts, and statements only to trigger a desire to search deeper into the art of musical expression. The greater depth for understanding such issues compliments our musical and instructional techniques.

Throughout my entire professional music-making career, musical expression was my prime focus. My goal is to share the beauty of music and to create greater meaning and appreciation to the art of music. The evidence to discover musical meaning can be found in the countless publications addressing musical expression. Some have gone to the point of documenting specific gestures intended to be used while conducting an ensemble. I can't imagine taking the time to learn such details that end up as being programmed events for specific compositions. Moreover, no two conductors can make identical gestures that flow with the same grace and poise. If this were the case, which one would be the imitator? I stress the importance for conductors to create their personal expressive gestures that flow with finesse and elegance, and are comfortable for one's conducting body-language.

As a conductor educator, I commend you for the massive contribution and guidance you are providing for so many musicians, students, and audience members. You compliment your community as they experience the language of musical expression. As stated earlier, beauty, compassion, appreciation, self-esteem, cooperation, and respect are but a few **life** and **living** priorities that are hidden in music study and performance. Music is a powerful force in humanity that cannot be denied. We search for expression and creative opportunities to share with others to satisfy our need for communication and appreciation. Through the fine art of music, our depth of beauty is sensitized by the nuance, inflection, and subtleties of rhythmic and lyrical expression. Being able to recognize and respond to music's fine art of detail enhances understanding and value appreciation that compliments our society.

Enjoy the beautiful world of music!

It is the I that holds the answer . . .

It is the I that cannot be copied, imitated, or contrived . . .

The I is found in the Intangible,

Intrinsic, Inherent, and the Innate.

The I words are connected through musical Imagination . . .

A musical imagination that speaks through the beauty of sound . . .

. . . moving in and out of silence!

Bibliography

Battisti, F. (2007). *On Becoming a Conductor*. Meredith Music Publications, distributed by Hal Leonard, Inc.

Blum, D. (1977). *Casals and the Art of Interpretation*. University of California Press.

Copland, A. (1980). *Music and Imagination*. Harvard University Press.

Csikszentmihalyi, M. (1990). *Flow: The Psychology of Optimal Experience*. Harper Perennial

Csikszentmihalyi, M. (1997). *Creativity: Psychology of Discovery & Invention*. Harper Perennial

Jordan, J. (1999). *The Musician's Soul*. GIA Publications.

Levitin, D. (2007). *This Is Your Brain on Music*. Plume/Penguin Group, Inc.

Sloboda, J. (2005). *Exploring the Musical Mind*. Oxford University Press.

Sokolowski, E. (2012). *Making Musical Meaning*. GIA Publications

Lisk. E. (2006). *The Creative Director: Conductor, Teacher, Leader*. Meredith Music Publications, distributed by Hal Leonard, Inc.

Lisk. E. (2010). *The Musical Mind of the Creative Director*. Meredith Music Publications, distributed by Hal Leonard, Inc.

Lisk E. (1996). *The Intangibles of Musical Performance*, Meredith Music Publications, distributed by Hal Leonard, Inc.

McGill, D. (2007). *Sound in Motion*. Indiana University Press

Walker, M. (2012). *The Art of Interpretation*. GIA Publications

Whitwell, D. *Essay: Music Education for the Future*, http://www.whitwellessays.com/

About the Author

EDWARD S. LISK is an internationally recognized clinician, conductor, and author. He is an honored and elected member (48th) of the prestigious *National Band Hall of Fame for Distinguished Conductors*. Mr. Lisk joins the ranks of notable conductors such as John Philip Sousa, Edwin Franko Goldman, Henry Fillmore, Col. Arnald Gabriel, and Col. John R. Bourgeois, among many others. He is a recipient of the distinguished *2009 Midwest Medal of Honor*. The *Midwest Medal of Honor* recognizes the recipients for their conspicuous efforts, worldwide recognition, and continuing influence in the development and improvement of instrumental ensembles. He recently was selected to receive the *2012 Phi Beta Mu International Outstanding Contributor to Bands Award*.

Called a "unique leader in the profession" and "a dynamic force in music education," Edward S. Lisk has been invited to speak and conduct throughout the United States and abroad. He is an inducted member of the prestigious *American Bandmasters Association* and in the year 2000, served as the 63rd President of this distinguished organization founded by Edwin Franko Goldman. His active guest-conducting schedule includes all-state bands, honor bands, university and professional bands. Since 1985, Mr. Lisk has served as an adjunct professor, appeared as a clinician/lecturer, adjudicator, and guest conductor throughout 85 universities in 46 states, five

Canadian Provinces and Australia. He is the author of *The Creative Director Series* (9 pub.) published by Meredith Music Publications, a coauthor of the highly acclaimed 9-volume publication by GIA, *Teaching Music Through Performance in Band* and editor of the *Edwin Franko Goldman March Series* for Carl Fischer Music Publications.

Mr. Lisk serves as Vice President of the *Midwest Clinic Board of Directors*, and President and CEO of the *John Philip Sousa Foundation*. He is a past-president of the *National Band Association* ('90–'92) and served NBA as Executive Secretary Treasurer ('97–'02). He is the recipient of many distinguished awards and titles.

Additional titles in this series published by Meredith Music Publications:

The Musical Mind of The Creative Director
Copyright © 2010
ISBN: 978-1-57463-160-9

The Creative Director: Conductor, Teacher, Leader
Copyright © 2006
ISBN: 1-57463-079-2

The Creative Director: Intangibles of Musical Performance
Copyright © 1996
ISBN: 0-9624308-5-4

The Creative Director: Alternative Rehearsal Techniques
Copyright © 1991
ISBN: 0-9624308-0-3

The Creative Director: Beginning and Intermediate Levels
Copyright © 2001
ISBN: 0-634-03044-2

Student Supplement Book I
Copyright © 1993
ISBN: 0-9624308-1-1

Student Supplement Book II
Copyright © 1994
ISBN: 0-9624308-2-X

The Creative Director: Alternative Rehearsal Techniques Teaching Accessories
Copyright © 1995
ISBN: 0-9624308-3-8

DVD: Alternative Rehearsal Techniques
Virginia Commonwealth University Wind Ensemble
Edward S. Lisk, Clinician; Dr. Terry Austin, Director
Copyright © 1994
ISBN: 0-9624308-4-6

The Creative Director Series publications are distributed by:
Hal Leonard Corp.
7777 West Bluemound Rd.
Milwaukee, WI 53213
414-774-3630
www.meredithmusic.com